Marion Richardson Drury

Our Catechism

a manual of Christian teaching for use in the families, Sunday schools,

junior societies, and juvenile missionary and temperance organizations of

the United Brethren in Christ

Marion Richardson Drury

Our Catechism

a manual of Christian teaching for use in the families, Sunday schools, junior societies, and juvenile missionary and temperance organizations of the United Brethren in Christ

ISBN/EAN: 9783337375072

Printed in Europe, USA, Canada, Australia, Japan

Cover: Foto ©Lupo / pixelio.de

More available books at **www.hansebooks.com**

A MANUAL OF CHRISTIAN TEACHING FOR USE IN THE
FAMILIES, SUNDAY SCHOOLS, JUNIOR SOCIETIES,
AND JUVENILE MISSIONARY AND TEMPER-
ANCE ORGANIZATIONS

OF THE

UNITED BRETHREN IN CHRIST

BY MARION R. DRURY, D.D.

DAYTON, OHIO
UNITED BRETHREN PUBLISHING HOUSE
1897

ACTION OF THE GENERAL CONFERENCE OF 1897.

THAT the General Conference authorize the trustees of the Printing Establishment to have prepared and published a Church catechism that shall cover Bible history and teaching, and our Church history, doctrines, and government, and that it be published at the earliest convenience.

ACTION OF THE BOOK COMMITTEE.

We, the Book Committee of the United Brethren Church, having carefully examined the manuscript submitted to us by Rev. M. R. Drury, D.D., find the subject matter to be, in our judgment, just such a catechism as was ordered by the General Conference, and believe the same to be well adapted, as such, to meet the demands and foster the best interests of our Church, and, therefore, give to it our hearty approval.

I. L. KEPHART.
H. A. THOMPSON.
E. LORENZ.
W. R. FUNK.

PREFACE.

For many years there has been a growing demand among pastors and other religious teachers in the United Brethren Church for a catechism, to be used in the Christian instruction and training of the children and young people of the denomination. This demand took definite shape and found specific expression at the General Conference held at Toledo, Iowa, in May, 1897, when a catechism was authorized to embrace both a manual of Bible history and teaching and the history and doctrines of the Church. With a view to meet these ends this manual has been prepared. It is intended for use by parents, Sunday-school teachers, pastors, and other leaders of juvenile Christian societies.

The word "catechism" has a well-understood meaning, and yet many seem to have a strong aversion to it. It has reference to a form of teaching by means of questions and answers. A catechism contains a summary of elementary principles or teachings reduced to this form. A church catechism would be a manual containing a summary of the essential teachings of a religious denomination.

The object of catechetical instruction is not thereby merely to fit those taught for church membership, but to give them a thorough knowledge of the fundamental doctrines of our holy religion. They cannot be educated into the kingdom of God; they must be born into it by the agency of the word of God and of the Holy Spirit. But having been converted, or with a view to their early conversion, children will be greatly benefited by careful instruction in the essential doctrines of the Bible and the Church. In the times of Christ and the apostles, and in the primitive church, this was a common method of teaching. That teaching by means of questions and answers is an effective way of inculcating truth no successful teacher of the young has any doubt. The church of to-day, while guarding well against its possible abuses, will do well more generally to avail itself of the helpful aid of the catechism. This is especially true in view of the widely prevalent interest that distinguishes this age in the organization of juvenile societies for Christian instruction and culture. Catechetical teaching is, therefore, not to be regarded so much as an end as it is a means to that thorough grounding in the truth that is so potent in promoting intelligent Christian living.

A church catechism of practical value must necessarily be limited in size and contents. It would, however, be essentially lack-

iii

ing in merit if it did not contain the leading truths which lie at
the foundation of all Christian belief. These are, for example,
the doctrines concerning God, concerning the person and work of
Jesus Christ, concerning the office and ministry of the Holy
Spirit, concerning man's nature and need and destiny, concerning
the way of salvation — what it is to be a Christian, concerning
prayer, and concerning the privileges and benefits which are en-
joyed by the true children of God.

Dr. J. R. Miller, an exceedingly helpful writer for young people,
in referring to the importance and necessity of doctrines in the
religious training of the young in the upbuilding of their character and life, well says: "It should begin in the home. It may be
well to have a revival of catechism teaching. Suppose the children do not now understand the statements of truth in the answers, if the words are put into their memory they will stay there
and will shape their thoughts for all life. In the Sunday school,
too, teachers may with profit spend a portion of every lesson
period in setting forth some doctrine which lies in the passage, or
is suggested by it."

If this manual shall prove of real service to parents and
teachers in training the young to be strong, vigorous, and stable
Christians, the end sought in its preparation will have a happy
realization. It is the author's uppermost wish that it may
accomplish at least a humble part in advancing Christ's kingdom in the earth.

M. R. D.

Dayton, Ohio, August, 1897.

CONTENTS.

PART IV.

TEMPERANCE.

PART V.

SUPPLEMENTAL LESSONS.

SUGGESTIONS TO TEACHERS.

PASTORS, superintendents of Junior societies, and other teachers who use this catechism will find it necessary to adapt their teaching to the children composing their classes. Many questions will need fuller answers than those given. For example, the questions in Bible history should be accompanied with a fuller account of the leading characters named than is given. This will require careful preparation in order that the lessons may be made interesting and profitable.

When the doctrines of sin, Christ, and salvation are studied, an effort should be made to lead all the children taught to a personal acceptance of Christ as their Saviour. Do not make the lessons too long, but seek to have the children learn well whatever is undertaken. There are many things that very young children will not understand. Make these as plain as you can, but seek to have all learn word for word the answers to all questions.

The catechism on the Church, Missions, and Temperance can be made very interesting if teachers will thoroughly prepare themselves for their work. If an additional catechism on temperance is desired, that prepared by Julia Coleman, Bible House, New York (price, five cents), will be found very suggestive and helpful. The United Brethren Handbook will also prove of great value in the hands of teachers.

The memory passages in the Supplemental Lessons may mostly be used as responsive readings, if so desired. Let the children, however, commit the psalms named, the thirteenth chapter of I. Corinthians, and the Ten Commandments to memory, so that they can recite them without prompting. Let them also commit to memory the prayers, that they may use them as their own.

Remember, the value of the catechism will depend chiefly on those who use it as teachers. Let parents and all others who undertake to teach its lessons to the children under their care seek divine wisdom, that their work may be fruitful in leading the tender lambs of the home and the Church to perfect rest and security in the fold of the Good Shepherd.

OUR CATECHISM.

PART I.

THE BIBLE.

CHAPTER I.

BIBLE HISTORY.

1. What is the best book in the world?
The Holy Bible.

2. Why is it better than other books?
Because God is its author, and because it teaches us important lessons which we find nowhere else.

3. How did God give the Bible to man?
He inspired good men to write it. (II. Tim. 3:16.)

4. What is the Bible?
It is the revelation of the truth of God and a record of the will of God.

5. Of what does the Bible give the history?
The Bible gives the history of God's dealings with men while teaching them his holy will.

6. Into what two principal parts is the Bible divided?
The Old and the New Testament.

1. THE OLD TESTAMENT.

7. Into how many books or parts is the Old Testament divided?
Thirty-nine.

8. What are the first five books, and what are they called?
They are Genesis, Exodus, Leviticus, Numbers, and

Deuteronomy, and they are called the Pentateuch, or
the five books of Moses.

9. What are the next twelve books called?
They are the historical books, and are Joshua, Judges,
Ruth, I. and II. Samuel, I. and II. Kings, I. and II.
Chronicles, Ezra, Nehemiah, and Esther.

10. What are the five books that follow?
They are the poetical books — Job, Psalms, Proverbs,
Ecclesiastes, the Song of Solomon.

*11. What are the remaining books of the Old Testa-
ment called?*
The books of the prophets.

12. Into what two classes are these divided?
The major and minor prophets.

13. Which are the major prophets?
Isaiah, Jeremiah, Lamentations, Ezekiel, Daniel, —
five.

14. Which are the minor prophets?
Hosea, Joel, Amos, Obadiah, Jonah, Micah, Nahum,
Habakkuk, Zephaniah, Haggai, Zechariah, Malachi, —
twelve.

*15. With what event does the history of the Bible
begin?*
The creation of man nearly six thousand years ago.
(Gen. 1: 26.)

*16. Who are some of the most prominent men men-
tioned in the Old Testament?*
Adam, Enoch, Noah, Abraham, Jacob, Joseph, Moses,
Joshua, Gideon, Samuel, David, Solomon, Elijah, Isaiah,
and Daniel.

17. Who was Adam?
He was the first man. (Gen. 2: 7.)

18. Who was Enoch?
He was a good man who walked with God and was
taken to heaven without dying. (Gen. 5: 24.)

19. Who was Noah?

He was a preacher of righteousness at a time when there was great wickedness in the world. (Gen. 6:5, 8.)

20. What wonderful event occurred during Noah's lifetime?

God sent a great flood upon the earth that destroyed all the people except Noah and his family. (Gen. 6:17.)

21. Who was Abraham?

He was a man of great faith in God and was called the friend of God. (Gen. 15:6; Jas. 2:23.)

22. Who was Jacob?

He was the prince of God, and from him sprang the twelve tribes of Israel. (Gen. 32:28.)

23. Who was Joseph?

He was the favorite son of Jacob, was sold by his brothers to be a slave in Egypt, and there he became the preserver of his people. (Gen. 37:2; 47:11.)

24. Who was Moses?

He was the founder of the Hebrew nation, and was its leader and lawgiver for a period of forty years. (Ex. 2:10; 3:10.)

25. Who was Joshua?

He was the successor of Moses, and led the people of Israel across the Jordan into the promised land of Canaan. (Num. 27:18; Josh. 1:1, 2.)

26. Who was Gideon?

He was one of the greatest of the judges, and won a great battle with only three hundred men. (Judg. 6:11, 12; 7:18, 19.)

27. Who was Samuel?

He was the last and the most honored of the judges, having been consecrated to the Lord from the time he was a little child. (I. Sam. 1:20; 7:15.)

28. Who was David?

He was the second king of Israel, and the writer of most of the Psalms. (I. Sam. 17:12-14; II. Sam. 2:4.)

29. *Who was Solomon?*

He was the son of David, and a very wise and rich king, but he did not rule to please God. (I. Ki. 1 : 33, 34.)

30. *Who was Elijah?*

He was a prophet of the Lord, and, like Enoch, was taken to heaven without death. (I. Ki. 17 : 1; II. Ki, 2 : 11.)

31. *Who was Isaiah?*

He was the greatest of the prophets, and wrote much about Christ seven hundred years before he came into the world. (Isa. 1 : 1.)

32. *Who was Daniel?*

He was a brave and true temperance boy, and when he became a man he was a prophet of the Lord, and because he prayed daily to his God he was cast into a den of lions. (Dan. 1: 8; 6 : 16.)

33. *Who are some of the most noted women mentioned in the Old Testament?*

Miriam, Ruth, Hannah, and Esther.

34. *Who was Miriam?*

She was the sister of Moses, and she sang a beautiful song of praise to God after the people of Israel had crossed the Red Sea. (Ex. 15: 20, 21.)

35. *Who was Ruth?*

She was a Moabitess who through her mother-in-law, Naomi, learned to love God and his people, and who was afterwards greatly honored of the Lord. (Ruth 1 : 1-4.)

36. *Who was Hannah?*

She was the mother of the good judge, Samuel. (I. Sam. 1 : 20.)

37. *Who was Esther?*

She was a Jewish woman, the wife of the king of Persia, and at one time she risked her own life to save the lives of her people. (Esth. 2: 17; 4: 16.)

38. *How many years does the history of the Old Testament embrace?*

Over four thousand.

2. The New Testament

39. Into how many parts or books is the New Testament divided?
Twenty-seven.

40. Into what three classes are these divided?
Into historical, doctrinal, and prophetical books.

41. Which of these are the historical books?
Matthew, Mark, Luke, John, and the Acts of the Apostles, — five.

42. Which are the doctrinal books?
Romans, I. and II. Corinthians, Galatians, Ephesians, Philippians, Colossians, I. and II. Thessalonians, I. and II. Timothy, Titus, Philemon, Hebrews, James, I. and II. Peter, I., II., and III. John, and Jude, — twenty-one.

43. Which is the only prophetical book?
Revelation, the last book in the Bible.

44. With what event does New Testament history begin?
The birth of Jesus Christ. (Matt. 2: 1.)

45. Who is Jesus Christ?
The only begotten Son of God. (John 1: 14.)

46. What books contain his history?
Matthew, Mark, Luke, and John.

47. What are these books called?
The four Gospels.

48. Why are they so called?
Because they contain the record of the life, works, and teachings of Jesus.

49. What are the chief events in his life?
His presentation in the temple when he was eight days old, his visit to Jerusalem at the age of twelve, his baptism at the age of thirty, his crucifixion at the age of thirty-three, his resurrection and ascension.

50. By whom was Jesus baptized?
John the Baptist, who was the forerunner of Jesus. Matt. 3: 13.)

51. *What are some of the chief things Jesus did during his public ministry?*

He taught the people, healed the sick, cast out evil spirits, and raised the dead to life.

52. *Whom did he choose and send out to preach his gospel?*

Twelve apostles. (Mark 3 : 14.)

53. *What are their names?*

Peter, James, John, Andrew, Philip, Bartholomew, Matthew, Thomas, James the Less, Thaddæus, Simon the Canaanite, and Judas Iscariot. (Mark 3 : 16-19.)

54. *What was the great commission Jesus gave to these twelve men?*

"Go ye into all the world, and preach the gospel to every creature" (Mark 16 : 15).

55. *Who was afterwards called to be an apostle?*

Paul.

56. *Who were the two chief preachers in the apostolic band?*

Peter and Paul.

57. *What great work did Peter do?*

He preached a sermon on the day of Pentecost that resulted in the conversion of three thousand souls. (Acts 2.)

58. *For what is Paul noted?*

As the apostle to the Gentiles and the first foreign missionary. (Acts 21 : 19; 16 : 9.)

59. *How long a period is included in the history of the New Testament?*

About one hundred years.

60. *Why is this history of so great importance to the world?*

Because it is the story of the life and work of Jesus Christ and of the beginnings of his kingdom among men.

CHAPTER II.

BIBLE TEACHINGS.

1. About God.

61. What is the first thing the Bible tells us about God?
That he is the creator of all things. (Gen. 1: 1.)

62. What is God?
God is a Spirit, and he is almighty, all-wise, eternal, and is everywhere present, beholding the evil and the good. (John 4: 24.)

63. What is the character of God?
God is holy, just, and good, and he is full of mercy, love, and truth. (Ex. 4: 6.)

64. Is there more than one God?
There is but one true God. (Isa. 44: 8; I. Cor. 8: 6.)

65. What is meant by the Trinity?
By the Trinity is meant the unity of three persons in one Godhead—the Father, the Son, and the Holy Spirit.

66. How are we to understand that these three persons are one?
They are of but one substance, and are equal in power and glory.

67. What is God's work in providence?
This triune God not only created the heavens and the earth and all that in them is, but he sustains, protects, and governs these with a gracious regard for the good of man and the glory of his name.

2. About Man.

68. How did man come to be in this world?
God created him. (Gen. 1: 26.)

69. *What are the two parts of man's being?*
The body and the soul.

70. *Of what did God make man's body?*
"Of the dust of the ground" (Gen. 2: 7).

71. *How did God make man's soul?*
He breathed into his nostrils the breath of life, and man became a living soul. (Gen. 2: 7.)

72. *What is the difference between the body and the soul?*
The body is material and must die; the soul is spiritual and must live forever.

73. *In whose image was man created?*
"God created man in his own image, in the image of God created he him" (Gen. 1: 27).

74. *What is meant by being created in the image of God?*
Having the spiritual nature of God and being like him in righteousness and true holiness. (Eph. 4: 24.)

75. *What dignity has God thus given to man?*
He is the crowning work of all his creation.

76. *What authority was given to man at his creation?*
God gave him dominion over every living thing. (Gen. 1: 28.)

77. *When man was created what law was given him?*
The law of perfect obedience to the will of God. (Gen. 2: 16, 17.)

78. *Did our first parents in Eden always obey this law?*
They violated it, and so brought sin into the world. (Gen. 3: 6.)

79. *What is sin?*
Sin is the transgression of the law of God, or the failure to conform to its holy requirements. (I. John 3: 4.)

80. *Who tempted our first parents to sin?*
Satan, the evil spirit. (Gen. 3: 1.)

81. What was the result of their sin?

They lost the image of God in which they had been created, and thus fell from their happy estate, becoming subject to pain and death. (Gen. 3: 16, 17.)

82. Did their sin affect any besides themselves?

Having become sinners, they transmitted to their posterity a sinful nature, so that all mankind was brought into an estate of sin and misery. (Rom. 5: 12-18.)

83. Can God be well pleased with his creatures who are sinful by nature and in life?

Sin is so displeasing to God that he cannot look upon it with any allowance. (Hab. 1: 13.)

3. ABOUT CHRIST.

84. Does God then not love sinners?

He loves sinners, but not their sins.

85. How did God show his love for sinful man?

"God so loved the world, that he gave his only begotten Son, that whosoever believeth in him should not perish, but have everlasting life" (John 3: 16).

86. What did the Son of God do to save sinners?

He came down from heaven, became a man, lived, died, and rose again.

87. How did Christ, being the Son of God, become man?

He took upon him the form of a servant, and was made in the likeness of man, having a human body and soul. (Phil. 2: 7, 8.)

88. Was Christ's life free from sin?

He was himself without sin, setting us a perfect example of goodness and holiness. (I. Pet. 2: 22.)

89. What did Christ do to redeem us from sin?

"He humbled himself, and became obedient unto death, even the death of the cross" (Phil. 2: 8).

90. Was it necessary that he should thus die for us?

Thus it behooved Christ to suffer, that he might make full atonement for our sins. (Luke 24: 46.)

2

91. Did Christ die for all men?

By the grace of God he tasted death for every man.
(Heb. 2: 9.)

92. Will all then be saved?

No ; only those will be saved who accept the salvation
Christ has provided. If they will cling to their sins, and
reject his salvation, they will be forever lost. (Ps.
9 : 17.)

93. What must we do to be saved?

Repent of our sins and believe on the Lord Jesus
Christ as our personal Saviour. (Acts 3 : 19; 16: 31.)

94. What is repentance?

It is such a sorrow for sin as leads us to turn from sin
unto God. (II. Cor. 7: 10.)

95. What is faith in Jesus Christ?

Faith in Jesus Christ is such a belief in him as enables
us to receive him and to trust in him alone for salvation.
(John 1: 12.)

96. Can we repent and believe without God's help?

The power to repent of our sins and to believe the gospel is given us of God. (Eph. 2 : 8; Rom. 11: 29.)

4. ABOUT SALVATION.

97. How may we know when we have saving faith?

"He that believeth on the Son of God hath the witness
in himself" (I. John 5: 10).

98. What witness is this?

"The Spirit itself beareth witness with our spirit, that
we are the children of God" (Rom. 8 : 16)

99. What are the benefits of salvation?

Justification, regeneration, adoption, and sanctification, and whatever blessings flow from these.

100. What is justification?

Justification is that act of God's grace whereby our
sins are pardoned, and we are accounted righteous for
Christ's sake. (Acts 13 : 39.)

101. *What is regeneration?*
Regeneration is the new birth of the soul whereby we are made alive to God and are enabled to live for him. (Tit. 3 : 5.)

102. *What is adoption?*
Adoption is that act of God's grace whereby we become members of his family. (Gal. 3 : 26; John 1 : 12.)

103. *What is sanctification?*
Sanctification is the work of God's grace, through the word and the Spirit, whereby we are made holy in heart and life. (II. Thes. 2: 13.)

104. *What other benefits do those share who have been saved from sin?*
The assurance of God's love, peace of conscience, joy in the Holy Ghost, and the hope of eternal glory.

105. *What is it to be a true Christian?*
To love God with all the heart and soul, mind and strength, and our neighbor as ourselves. (Matt. 22: 37-40.)

106. *When once saved, how shall we keep from again falling into sin?*
By continual watchfulness, the study of God's word, prayer, and a life of faith in the Son of God. (Mark 4 : 38.)

5. ABOUT CHRISTIAN LIVING.

107. *When one has become a Christian, what is his chief business?*
To live for Christ. (II. Cor. 5 : 15.)

108. *How are we to live for him?*
By seeking to do his will in all things.

109. *Where do we find his will?*
In the Bible, which contains the moral law.

110. *Where is the moral law found?*
In the Decalogue, or Ten Commandments.

(1) THE TEN COMMANDMENTS.

111. What is the first commandment?
"Thou shalt have no other gods before me."

112. What is meant by this commandment?
That there is but one God, and that we are to fear, love, and trust in him alone.

113. What is the second commandment?
"Thou shalt not make unto thee any graven image, or any likeness of any thing that is in heaven above, or that is in the earth beneath, or that is in the water under the earth : thou shalt not bow down thyself to them, nor serve them : for I the Lord thy God am a jealous God, visiting the iniquity of the fathers upon the children unto the third and fourth generation of them that hate me; and showing mercy unto thousands of them that love me, and keep my commandments."

114. What is meant by this commandment?
That we are not to make or bow down to any false gods.

115. What is the third commandment?
"Thou shalt not take the name of the Lord thy God in vain: for the Lord will not hold him guiltless that taketh his name in vain."

116. What is meant by this commandment?
We should so love and fear God as not to profane his holy name by swearing, or by using it in any light or thoughtless way.

117. What is the fourth commandment?
"Remember the Sabbath day, to keep it holy. Six days shalt thou labor, and do all thy work : but the seventh day is the Sabbath of the Lord thy God : in it thou shalt not do any work, thou, nor thy son, nor thy daughter, thy man-servant, nor thy maid-servant, nor thy cattle, nor thy stranger that is within thy gates: for in six days the Lord made heaven and earth, the sea, and all that in them is, and rested the seventh day: wherefore the Lord blessed the Sabbath day, and hallowed it."

118. What is meant by this commandment?

That the day which God has appointed as the Sabbath should be observed as a day of holy rest and of religious meditation and worship.

119. What is the fifth commandment?

"Honor thy father and thy mother: that thy days may be long upon the land which the Lord thy God giveth thee."

120. What is meant by this commandment?

That we should so love and cherish our parents that we will give them due honor and obedience.

121. What is the sixth commandment?

"Thou shalt not kill."

122. What is meant by this commandment?

That God places great value upon human life, and we are not to take it unjustly at any time.

123. What is the seventh commandment?

"Thou shalt not commit adultery."

124. What is meant by this commandment?

That we are not to indulge in any unchaste thoughts, words, or actions, but to live a life of strict purity.

125. What is the eighth commandment?

"Thou shalt not steal."

126. What is meant by this commandment?

That we shall not rob our neighbor of his money or property, or take anything from him by unfair means.

127. What is the ninth commandment?

"Thou shalt not bear false witness against thy neighbor."

128. What is meant by this commandment?

That we should always so honor the truth that we will not belie, slander, or in any way speak evil of our neighbor to do him injury.

129. What is the tenth commandment?

"Thou shalt not covet thy neighbor's house, thou shalt not covet thy neighbor's wife, nor his man-servant, nor his maid-servant, nor his ox, nor his ass, nor any thing that is thy neighbor's."

130. What is meant by this commandment?

That we are to so love our neighbor that we will not envy him his property or his good fortune, or wrongfully seek to gain possession of anything that is his.

131. What does our Saviour give as the sum of these commandments?

"Thou shalt love the Lord thy God with all thy heart, and with all thy soul, and with all thy mind. This is the first and great commandment. And the second is like unto it, Thou shalt love thy neighbor as thyself. On these two commandments hang all the law and the prophets" (Matt. 24 : 37-40).

132. What is the Golden Rule?

"All things whatsoever ye would that men should do to you, do ye even so to them" (Matt. 7 : 12).

133. How are all these commandments to be observed?

They are to be observed in thought as well as in deed. (Matt. 5 : 21, 22, 27, 28.)

134. Are we able so to keep them in our own strength?

We are not, for apart from the grace of God in Christ Jesus our Saviour no one can perfectly obey the law of God.

135. How then may we keep God's law?

We are to take Jesus Christ, who himself perfectly obeyed the whole law, as our Saviour, and trust constantly in his forgiving love and saving grace. (I. John 3 : 5.)

(2) PRAYER.

136. What is one of the principal means God has ordained to aid us in keeping his commandments?

Prayer.

137. What is prayer?

Prayer is the offering up of our desires to God for things agreeable to his holy will.

138. *What else belongs to true prayer?*
The confession of our sins, thanksgiving for God's mercies, and faith in his promises.

139. *Has God promised to hear our prayers?*
He has promised to always hear and answer the prayer of faith. (Matt. 7 : 7.)

140. *What rule of prayer is given us in the Bible?*
The prayer Christ taught his disciples, called the Lord's Prayer.

141. *What is this prayer that teaches us to pray?*
"Our Father which art in heaven, Hallowed be thy name. Thy kingdom come. Thy will be done in earth, as it is in heaven. Give us this day our daily bread. And forgive us our debts, as we forgive our debtors. And lead us not into temptation, but deliver us from evil: for thine is the kingdom, and the power, and the glory, for ever. Amen."

142. *What is meant by the words " Our Father which art in heaven"?*
That we are to think of God when we pray with filial gratitude as our Heavenly Father.

143. *How many petitions are there in this model prayer?*
There are six—three that relate to God, and three that relate to man.

144. *What is the first petition?*
"Hallowed be thy name."

145. *What is meant by this petition?*
That we should think of God as holy, and seek his glory in all things.

146. *What is the second petition?*
"Thy kingdom come."

147. *What is meant by this petition?*
That God has a spiritual kingdom which we would have him set up in our hearts and in the world.

148. What is the third petition?
"Thy will be done in earth, as it is in heaven."

149. What is meant by this petition?
That we may know and do the will of God in all things, as the angels do it in heaven.

150. What is the fourth petition?
"Give us this day our daily bread."

151. What is meant by this petition?
This is a prayer for the continuance of our life and strength, that we may be able to do God's will and service.

152. What is the fifth petition?
"Forgive us our debts, as we forgive our debtors."

153. What is meant by this petition?
This prayer teaches us that forgiveness is as needful for the soul as bread is for the body, and that if we would find forgiveness of God we must be loving and forgiving to our fellow-men.

154. What is the sixth petition?
"Lead us not into temptation, but deliver us from evil."

155. What is meant by this petition?
That having cast upon our Heavenly Father all the cares of our earthly life, and having been freed from the burden of sin, we need to be led by God's own hand that we fall not into temptation and evil.

156. What is the conclusion of the Lord's Prayer?
"For thine is the kingdom, and the power, and the glory, for ever. Amen."

157. What does this teach us?
That the hope for the answer of our prayer is in the Lord only, and therefore that we should ever keep before us the thought of his kingdom, his power, and his glory.

158. What is meant by the word "Amen"?
As we pray, so be it, Lord.

6. About Death and Eternity.

159. *What is death?*

It is the end of our earthly life, when the soul is separated from the body.

160. *Where do our souls go at death?*

The souls of the righteous go to heaven, and the souls of the wicked to hell.

161. *What becomes of our bodies after death?*

They lie in the grave till the resurrection, at the last day, when Christ shall come to raise the dead.

162. *Will all the dead be raised?*

"There shall be a resurrection of the dead, both of the just and the unjust" (John 5: 28, 29; Acts 24: 15).

163. *Will all men be judged at the last day?*

"We must all appear before the judgment seat of Christ; that every one may receive the things done in his body, according to that he hath done, whether it be good or bad" (II. Cor. 5: 10).

164. *What will then become of the wicked and the righteous?*

The wicked shall go away into everlasting punishment; but the righteous into life eternal. (Matt. 25: 46.)

165. *What is heaven?*

Heaven is the everlasting home God will give to all his true children after death. (John 14: 2, 3.)

166. *What is the preparation we need for heaven?*

We must be pure in heart and live a life of love and service to Jesus Christ our Saviour, who loved us and gave himself for us. (Matt. 5: 8; Gal. 2: 20.)

167. *Do we know when death will come to us?*

We do not, but we are sure it will come to all. (Eccl. 8: 8; Rom. 5: 12.)

168. *How, then, shall we be ready for death and a happy eternity?*

"Be thou faithful unto death, and I will give thee a crown of life." (Rev. 2 : 10.)

PART II.

The Church.

CHAPTER III.

THE CHURCH OF CHRIST.

1. What institution was founded by Christ and his apostles?

The church.

2. What is the church?

The church is the body of believers who confess that Jesus of Nazareth is the Christ of God. (Matt. 16: 16, 18.)

3. In how many forms does the church exist?

Two; the visible and the invisible.

4. Of what is the visible church composed?

The general body of Christian believers, in which the word of God is taught in its purity, the sacraments are duly administered, and the worship of God is maintained.

5. Of what is the invisible church composed?

Of all God's true children in all ages and in all places.

6. How does Christ regard his church?

He loves it, and has promised that the gates of hell shall never prevail against it. (Matt. 16: 18.)

7. Why should all Christian believers be members of the visible church?

Because by joining the church and working for it they show their love for Christ and the spiritual home he has provided for them.

8. What preparation does one need to join the church?

A deep sense of the need of Christ as a personal Saviour and a hearty acceptance of him.

9. *What are the sacraments of the church?*
Baptism and the Lord's Supper.

10. *What is a sacrament?*
A sacrament is a holy ordinance instituted by Christ, and is an outward and visible sign of an inward and spiritual grace.

11. *What is baptism?*
Baptism is a sacrament wherein water is applied to the one receiving it, in the name of the Father, the Son, and the Holy Ghost, and signifies the acceptance of the covenant of grace in Christ Jesus.

12. *Are any to be baptized but believers in Christ?*
The children of believing parents may be baptized, the parents thereby making a solemn covenant to bring them up in the nurture and admonition of the Lord.

13. *What advantages are shared by baptized persons?*
By baptism believers are admitted into the visible church of Christ, and children are thereby recognized as embraced in the covenant of grace in Christ Jesus, and the special subjects of his love and care.

14. *What is the Lord's Supper?*
The Lord's Supper is a sacrament in which bread and wine are used according to Christ's appointment, to keep in memory his sufferings and death for our sins. (I. Cor. 11 : 23, 26.)

15. *What preparation do we need to receive this holy sacrament?*
A true faith in Jesus Christ as our Saviour and a sincere desire to please him in all things.

CHAPTER IV.

THE UNITED BRETHREN CHURCH.

16. What are the different divisions or branches of the one church of Christ called?

They are called churches or denominations.

17. What is the church with which we are connected called?

The United Brethren in Christ.

1. OUTLINE HISTORY.

18. What reasons can we give for our connection with this Church?

It was providentially founded, and in the providence of God we have become connected with it, or have chosen its fellowship and service for the appointed purposes of the church of God.

19. When was the United Brethren Church founded?

The first regular annual conference was held in 1800. A revival movement leading up to this organization had been in progress for more than thirty years.

20. Who were the first members of the Church?

They were Germans settled in America who were destitute of the preaching of the gospel, or who were formal and without vital Christianity, but were awakened and converted under the earnest preaching of godly men.

21. Who were the leaders in the founding of the Church?

William Otterbein, a minister of the German Reformed Church, who came as a missionary from Germany in 1752, and Martin Boehm, a spiritual preacher of the Mennonites.

28

22. Where did the Church originate?

In Pennsylvania, Maryland, and Virginia, but it has since extended to all parts of the United States and to Canada, and has missions in Africa, China, Japan, and also in Germany.

23. What are some of the characteristics of the Church?

It is evangelical and evangelistic, and combines the prominent features of the various forms of church government.

24. What are the departments of Church work?

Missions, church erection, Sabbath schools, publishing, education, and young people's work.

2. Special Privileges and Duties.

25. What are the privileges and duties of the children and young people of the Church?

To study the Word of God in the Sunday school and to take part in the religious services of Junior and other young people's societies.

26. What are some of the helps to the formation of good character and leading to a life of usefulness?

The reading of good books and papers, the use of the various means of education, and the daily performance of noble and upright acts.

27. What relation does the home have to the church?

The home and the church are closely related, both being of divine origin, and have in view the best interests of society.

28. What does our Church teach about family religion?

Parents should never omit to pray with their families, morning and evening, and to set them a good example in all the Christian virtues.

29. What is the duty of pastors as to the home training of children?

They are publicly to teach the people what God's Word declares respecting the duty of parents to train up their children in the love and fear of the Lord.

30. How may children be profited by the godly teachings of their parents?

By giving heed to what is taught them and by obedience to their parents in all rightful things.

3. THE CONFESSION OF FAITH.

31. What is the brief statement of the leading doctrines of the United Brethren Church called?

The Confession of Faith.

32. Of what does this Confession consist?

Of thirteen articles.

33. When was the Confession in its present form adopted?

In 1889.

34. What is the preface to the Confession of Faith?

"In the name of God, we declare and confess before all men the following articles of our belief."

35. What is the first article?

"We believe in the only true God, the Father, the Son, and the Holy Ghost; that these three are one—the Father in the Son, the Son in the Father, and the Holy Ghost equal in essence or being with the Father and the Son."

36. What is meant by this article?

We believe that there is only one God, but that there are three persons in the Godhead—the Father, the Son, and the Holy Ghost, and that these comprise the Holy Trinity.

37. What is the second article?

"We believe that this triune God created the heavens and the earth, and all that in them is, visible and invisible; that he sustains, protects, and governs these, with gracious regard for the welfare of man, to the glory of his name."

38. What is meant by this article? ·

We believe that God created all things, and that he preserves and cares for all his creatures.

39. What is the third article?

"We believe in Jesus Christ; that he is very God and man; that he became incarnate by the power of the Holy Ghost and was born of the Virgin Mary; that he is the Saviour and Mediator of the whole human race, if they with full faith accept the grace proffered in Jesus; that this Jesus suffered and died on the cross for us, was buried, rose again on the third day, ascended into heaven, and sitteth on the right hand of God to intercede for us; and that he will come again at the last day to judge the living and the dead."

40. What is meant by this article?

We believe that Jesus Christ is a divine Saviour, and that all who sincerely believe in him have everlasting life.

41. What is the fourth article?

"We believe in the Holy Ghost; that he is equal in being with the Father and the Son; that he convinces the world of sin, of righteousness, and of judgment; that he comforts the faithful and guides them into all truth."

42. What is meant by this article?

We believe that the Holy Ghost is a divine person, and that without his help we shall not be able to find and walk in the ways of righteousness.

43. What is the fifth article?

"We believe that the Holy Bible, Old and New Testaments, is the word of God; that it reveals the only true way to our salvation; that every true Christian is bound to acknowledge and receive it by the help of the Spirit of God as the only rule and guide in faith and practice."

44. What is meant by this article?

We believe that God's Word reveals the only way of life, and that we ought to receive it with faith and love, lay it upon our hearts, and practice its precepts in our lives.

45. What is the sixth article?

"We believe in a holy Christian church, composed of

true believers, in which the word of God is preached by men divinely called, and the ordinances are duly administered; that this divine institution is for the maintenance of worship, for the edification of believers, and the conversion of the world to Christ."

46. What is meant by this article?

We believe that the church of Christ is a holy institution, and that all who love Christ should be members of it, and enjoy its gracious benefits.

47. What is the seventh article?

"We believe that the sacraments, Baptism and the Lord's Supper, are to be used in the Church, and should be practiced by all Christians; but the mode of baptism and the manner of observing the Lord's Supper are always to be left to the judgment and understanding of each individual. Also, the baptism of children shall be left to the judgment of believing parents."

48. What is meant by this article?

We believe that the sacraments of the New Testament should be observed by all believers in Christ, and that through them special spiritual blessings are bestowed.

49. What is the eighth article?

"We believe that man is fallen from original righteousness, and apart from the grace of our Lord Jesus Christ, is not only entirely destitute of holiness, but is inclined to evil, and only evil, and that continually; and that except a man be born again he cannot see the kingdom of heaven."

50. What is meant by this article?

We believe that we are all sinners by nature and practice, and that unless we are made alive unto God by the Holy Spirit we can never enter into the kingdom of God.

51. What is the ninth article?

"We believe that penitent sinners are justified before God only by faith in our Lord Jesus Christ, and not by works; yet that good works in Christ are acceptable to God, and spring out of a true and living faith."

52. What is meant by this article?

We believe that we can only be just in the eyes of the moral law when we accept Jesus Christ as our Saviour, who himself kept that law perfectly.

53. What is the tenth article?

"We believe that regeneration is the renewal of the heart of man after the image of God, through the word, by the act of the Holy Ghost, by which the believer receives the spirit of adoption and is enabled to serve God with the will and the affections."

54. What is meant by this article?

We believe that those who are born anew in the image of Christ are received into the family of God, and that they have all the rights and privileges of the children of God.

55. What is the eleventh article?

"We believe that sanctification is the work of God's grace, through the word and the Spirit, by which those who have been born again are separated in their acts, words, and thoughts from sin, and are enabled to live unto God, and to follow holiness, without which no man shall see the Lord.

56. What is meant by this article?

We believe that God requires all his children to be holy, and that we should strive by his help to live without willful sin.

57. What is the twelfth article?

"We believe that the Christian Sabbath is divinely appointed; that it is commemorative of our Lord's resurrection from the grave, and is an emblem of our eternal rest; that it is essential to the welfare of the civil community, and to the permanence and growth of the Christian church, and that it should be reverently observed as a day of holy rest and of social and public worship."

58. What is meant by this article?

We believe that the Sabbath is a holy day, set apart by God himself, for the good of our bodies and souls, and that on it we should refrain from all worldly pursuits and pleasures.

3

59. *What is the thirteenth article ?*

" We believe in the resurrection of the dead; the future general judgment; and an eternal state of rewards, in which the righteous dwell in endless life, and the wicked in endless punishment."

60. *What is meant by this article ?*

We believe that God will bring every one of us into judgment at the last day, for all we have done, whether good or bad, and that we should earnestly strive to be ready to enter into life, that we may be forever with the Lord.

PART III.

MISSIONS.

CHAPTER V.

ORIGIN AND PROGRESS OF CHRISTIAN MISSIONS.

1. What command did Jesus give to his disciples just before he ascended to heaven?

"Go ye into all the world, and preach the gospel to every creature" (Mark 16 : 15).

2. What does this mean?

That the disciples were to be missionaries to bear the gospel to others.

3. What is the true spirit of missions?

Love for Christ and the souls of men for whom he died.

4. What is the true aim of missionary work?

To make Christ known to the world.

5. How are missionaries sent out?

By churches and missionary societies.

6. Are there enough missionaries?

"The harvest truly is plenteous, but the laborers are few" (Matt. 9 : 37).

7. Do the heathen want the gospel?

Their cry to-day is the same as in the days of Paul the Apostle to the Gentiles, "Come over and help us."

8. Was Paul a missionary?

He was the first gospel missionary to a foreign land of whom we have any account.

9. Does the Lord care for the heathen?

He surely does, for he says, "Ask of me, and I shall

give thee the heathen for thine inheritance, and the uttermost parts of the earth for thy possession" (Ps. 2: 8).

10. *Is it our duty to pray for the heathen?*
"Pray ye therefore the Lord of the harvest, that he will send forth laborers into his harvest" (Matt. 9: 38.

11. *What would be a good missionary motto?*
Go or send.

12. *What does this mean?*
It means that we should go out as missionaries ourselves, or if we cannot go, that we will give of our money to send others.

13. *What promise of reward is made to those who go or send?*
They that turn many to righteousness shall shine as the stars forever and ever. (Dan. 12: 3.)

14. *When did the work of modern missions begin?*
In 1792, when William Carey was sent as a missionary to India.

15. *Who have been some of the leading missionaries of the nineteenth century, and where did they labor?*
William Carey, India; Robert Morrison, China; Adoniram Judson, Burmah; Robert Moffat, South Africa; David Livingstone, Africa; Robert McAll, France; Joseph Hardy Neesima, Japan.

16. *What has this century been called?*
The missionary century of the Christian era.

17. *What is the outlook for missionary endeavor in the twentieth century?*
The gospel will continue to spread till "the kingdoms of this world are become the kingdoms of our Lord and of his Christ."

CHAPTER VI.

MISSIONS OF THE UNITED BRETHREN CHURCH.

1. The General Board.

18. What has been peculiar to the United Brethren Church during all its history?
It has always had an earnest missionary spirit.

19. What can be said of its early ministers?
They were faithful and successful missionaries.

20. When was the Home, Frontier, and Foreign Missionary Society organized?
In 1853.

(1) AFRICA.

21. When was the first foreign mission established?
In 1855.

22. Where was the mission located?
At Sheugeh, West Africa, sixty miles south of Freetown, among the Sherbro people.

23. Who were the first missionaries?
W. J. Shuey, D. K. Flickinger, and D. C. Kumler.

24. What was the first work done?
Building a chapel and schoolroom.

25. When were the first converts in the mission reported?
In 1859, when Thomas Tucker, aged twenty, and Lucy Caulker, aged fourteen, a daughter of the chief, were happily converted.

26. What has been the progress of the work since?
Though slow at times, it has steadily advanced, showing constantly the blessing of God upon it.

27. *When was the first industrial school established ?*
In 1876.

28. *What school was founded in 1887 for the training of native workers for the mission ?*
The Theological Training-School, through the gift of Mr. Rufus Clark and wife, of Denver, Colorado.

29. *What missionary was longest in the service in this mission ?*
Rev. Joseph Gomer, who died September 5, 1892, having been twenty-two years an earnest and heroic missionary in the Dark Continent.

30. *What can be said of other missionaries in this field ?*
They have wrought well, and in the spirit of their Master, Jesus Christ, and they are held in deserved honor.

31. *What is the hope for this work in the future ?*
That it will continue to prosper in the hands of consecrated missionaries till Africa shall be brought to know Christ, the world's Saviour.

(2) GERMANY.

32. *When did the Church begin missionary work in Germany ?*
In 1869, under the labors of Rev. C. Bischoff, who was sent there from America.

33. *Why was a mission planted in that country ?*
Because it was the land of Otterbein, the founder of our Church, and because Germans in America who had found a new spiritual life under the preaching of the United Brethren had a burning desire that their friends in the home land might share their new-found joys.

34. *What are the evidences of the wisdom of this work ?*
The many that have been converted and the number of churches that have been established.

(3) JAPAN.

35. *When was the missionary work of the Church opened in Japan ?*
In 1895, with several native missionaries who had been educated in America.

36. What were the special encouragements to open the work in that country?

The eagerness of the people to adopt foreign customs, the religious freedom guaranteed by the government, and the readiness of cultured and consecrated missionaries to begin the work.

37. What results have been realized?

Many have been converted under the labors of the missionaries, and the future is full of hope.

(4) HOME MISSIONS.

38. What are home missions?

Missions in our own country.

39. Where are such missions operated by the United Brethren Church?

In numerous cities and towns throughout our country, east and west, north and south.

40. What has been the influence of the missionary work of the denomination on its life and growth?

The Church has been most active and has had its most rapid growth during the period of its greatest missionary activity.

41. Have foreign missions really paid?

The Church has never had a better investment, for it has always done the best for those at home when it has done its best for those far away.

2. THE WOMAN'S MISSIONARY ASSOCIATION.

42. When was the Woman's Missionary Association of the United Brethren Church organized?

In 1875.

43. Where are the missions of this society located?

In Africa, China, and at Portland, Oregon.

(1) AFRICA.

44. When and where was the first mission opened in Africa?

In 1877, at Rotufunk, on the Bompeh River, fifty miles southeast of Freetown.

45.   Who was the first missionary in charge of the work there?

Miss Emily Beeken, who, after nearly two years' work, was succeeded by other earnest and devoted workers.

46.   What losses has this mission sustained by death?

The loss of Rev. R. N. West, twelve years the superintendent of the mission, and of Miss Frankie Williams and Miss Elma Bittle, true and brave workers.

47.   What is the work done in the mission?

Preaching the gospel, conducting a medical dispensary, and operating an industrial and other schools and girls' and boys' homes, all of which is done with increasing good results from year to year.

(2)   CHINA.

48.   When was missionary work begun in China?

In 1889.

49.   Where was the mission located?

In Canton.

50.   Why was it located there?

Because it is the home of most of the Chinese in the United States, and the mission hopes to be able to secure the services of those converted here when they return to China.

51.   What is the character of the work being done in this mission?

It is evangelistic and educational, and has connected with it a successful medical dispensary.

52.   Do the Chinese want the gospel?

Many of them do after they come to know what it is and what it will do for them.

53.   What is China's greatest need?

Teachers and schools.

54.   What can we do to supply this need?

If we cannot go we can pray and give.

(3) PORTLAND, OREGON.

55. *When was the mission in this city opened?*
In 1883.

56. *What is the object of the mission?*
To conduct a school for the Chinese of this country, and through it secure their conversion to Christ, so that when they return to China they will be missionaries there among their own people.

57. *What has been done in this mission?*
More than a thousand Chinese have been in the school, and over one hundred have been converted, some of whom are now doing good work as missionaries.

CHAPTER VII.

MISSIONARY GIVING.

58. Where do we learn how to give for missions?
In the Bible.

59. What does it teach us is the first thing necessary to right giving?

That we give ourselves to the Lord to do his will. (II. Cor. 8 : 5; Isa. 6 : 8.)

60. What should be the rule of our giving?
"Thou shalt give unto the Lord thy God, according as the Lord thy God hath blessed thee" (Deut. 16 : 10).

61. How should we give?
"God loveth a cheerful giver" (II. Cor. 9 : 7).

62. When should we give?
"Upon the first day of the week let every one of you lay by him in store, as God hath prospered him" (I. Cor. 16 : 2).

63. How much should we give?
"Of all that thou shalt give me I will surely give the tenth unto thee" (Gen. 28 : 22).

64. With what motive should we give?
"Whatsoever ye do, do all to the glory of God" (I. Cor. 10 : 31).

65. Does Christ regard giving to help the heathen as giving to himself?
He does, for he says, "Inasmuch as ye have done it unto one of the least of these my brethren, ye have done it unto me" (Matt. 25 : 40).

PART IV.

TEMPERANCE.

CHAPTER VIII.

WHAT TEMPERANCE IS.

1. *What is temperance?*
Temperance is wise self-control, the moderate use of good things, and total abstinence from evil things.

2. *What is the most common form of intemperance?*
The use of intoxicating drinks.

1. ALCOHOLIC DRINKS AND THEIR FRUITS.

3. *What is it in strong drink that is so dangerous?*
Alcohol.

4. *What is alcohol?*
It is a liquid poison.

5. *Does temperance allow a moderate use of poisons?*
It does not, for poisons are injurious even in small quantities.

6. *What do we mean by strong drinks?*
Drinks that contain alcohol.

7. *Is there alcohol in cider, wines, and beer?*
While these drinks do not contain as much alcohol as some others, there is always some alcohol in them.

8. *Are they, therefore, dangerous?*
They are very dangerous, and many acquire the appetite for stronger liquors by using these drinks.

9. *What happens to the one who drinks alcoholic liquors?*
He gets drunk.

10. Why does he get drunk?

Because the alcohol is a poison that affects the brain and makes the one who drinks it crazy.

11. How is alcohol made?

It is made from grains or fruits that contain sugar, by the process of decay, or rotting.

12. Did God ever make alcohol?

No; it is one of the evil things man makes out of the good gifts of God.

13. Is alcohol good for anything?

It is not good to drink, though it is useful to burn.

14. Does the use of alcoholic drinks injure the body?

It weakens the body, injures the stomach, and often causes heart-disease and an early death.

15. Does drunkenness cause men to commit crime?

Yes, more than three-fourths of the crimes of the land are caused in some way by the use of intoxicating drinks.

16. Is the money that is spent for strong drink wasted?

It is worse than wasted, for it brings trouble and poverty and shame and death.

2. RESULTS OF ABSTINENCE.

17. What could be done if the money spent for strong drink were saved?

It would buy food, clothing, books, and a great many other good things.

18. What would be the result if all people would abstain from the use of strong drinks?

This would be a much better and happier world in which to live.

19. What can we do for temperance?

We should first of all learn how harmful alcohol is, and then we should never touch, taste, or handle it.

20. Should we all take a pledge to do this?

Yes, and the stronger the better.

21. What is the advantage of such a pledge?
Those who keep it will never have an appetite for strong drink, and so will never become drunkards.

3. THE CHURCH AND TEMPERANCE.

22. What has been the history of our Church on the temperance question?
The General Conference took advanced ground in favor of total abstinence in 1821, and the Church has ever since been loyal to that position.

23. What is the rule of the Church now respecting the use of intoxicating drinks?
The distilling, vending, and using of intoxicating drinks as a beverage are forbidden.

24. What more is forbidden?
Members of the Church are not permitted to rent or lease property for the manufacture or sale of such drinks, or to sign petitions for granting license, or to become bondsmen for persons engaged in the traffic in intoxicating drinks.

25. Does the Church permit even the moderate use of intoxicating drinks as a beverage?
It does not, but requires of all the practice of total abstinence.

26. Is the Church then a temperance society?
It is, and one of the best, and all who join it promise to practice the principles of temperance.

4. TOBACCO.

27. Is the use of tobacco a form of intemperance?
It is.

28. What is tobacco?
It is a poisonous plant.

29. How do you know it is poisonous?
Because it will make those not accustomed to its use sick when they take it into their mouths.

30. What is the effect of this poison?
It injures the bodies and minds of those who use it.

31. What form of the use of tobacco is especially harmful to boys?

Cigarette smoking.

32. What kind of a pledge ought all to take with respect to tobacco?

A pledge never to use it in any form.

33. What does our Church advise respecting the use of tobacco?

It advises all its members to wholly abstain from its use in every form.

34. Will the Church license persons to preach the gospel who use tobacco?

It will not.

35. What can we do to destroy this filthy, expensive, and harmful tobacco habit?

We can refuse to use it ourselves, and so set a good example to others.

CHAPTER IX.

THE BIBLE AND TEMPERANCE.

36. What does the Bible teach us about self-control?

That he is better "that ruleth his spirit than he that taketh a city" (Prov. 16 : 32).

37. What does this mean?

That the truest success in life requires self-mastery.

38. When should one learn to be master of himself?

When he is young.

39. Does the Bible speak of temperance children?

It tells of several who lived in Bible times.

40. What are some of their names?

Samuel and Samson, Daniel and his three friends, and John the Baptist.

41. How did Samuel become a total abstainer?

His mother taught him temperance principles and kept him pure until he was old enough to watch over himself.

42. Was she a strictly temperance woman?

She said to the priest: "I have drunk neither wine nor strong drink, but have poured out my soul before the Lord" (I. Sam. 1 : 15).

43. For what was Sampson noted?

His great strength.

44. What noble purpose had Daniel?

"But Daniel purposed in his heart that he would not defile himself with the portion of the king's meat, nor with the wine which he drank" (Dan. 1: 8).

45. Did the total abstinence of Daniel and his friends injure them?

"So he consented to them in this matter, and proved them ten days. And at the end of ten days their countenances appeared fairer and fatter in flesh than all the children which did eat the portion of the king's meat" (Dan. 1 : 14, 15).

46. How was John the Baptist honored?

He was a bright and shining light in the world and prepared the way for the coming and work of Jesus.

47. Does true temperance tend to success in life?

"Every man that striveth for the mastery is temperate in all things" (I. Cor. 9 : 25).

48. What is the fruit of the Spirit?

"The fruit of the Spirit is love, joy, peace, long-suffering, gentleness, goodness, faith, meekness, temperance" (Gal. 5 : 22, 23).

49. Why should we avoid strong drink?

Because "wine is a mocker, strong drink is raging; and whosoever is deceived thereby is not wise" (Prov. 20 : 1).

50. Why should we not associate with wine-drinkers?

"Be not among wine-bibbers; among riotous eaters of flesh; for the drunkard and the glutton shall come to poverty; and drowsiness shall clothe a man with rags" (Prov. 23 : 20, 21).

51. "Who hath woe? Who hath sorrow? Who hath contentions? Who hath babblings? Who hath wounds without cause? Who hath redness of eyes?" (Prov. 23 : 29.)

"They that tarry long at the wine; they that go to seek mixed wine" (Prov. 23 : 30).

52. How can we avoid these evils?

"Look not thou upon the wine when it is red, when it giveth his color in the cup, when it moveth itself aright" (Prov. 23 : 31).

53. What will be the result if not avoided?

"At the last it biteth like a serpent, and stingeth like an adder" (Prov. 23 : 32).

*54. Will an appetite for strong drink excuse the use
of it?*

"Woe unto them that rise up early in the morning,
that they may follow strong drink; that continue unto
night, until wine inflame them" (Isa. 5 : 11).

*55. Is there anything wrong in inducing others to use
strong drink?*

"Woe unto him that giveth his neighbor strong drink,
that putteth thy bottle to him, and makest him drunken
also" (Hab. 2 : 15).

*56. Does the good of others require us to abstain from
strong drink?*

"It is good neither to eat flesh, nor to drink wine, nor
any thing whereby thy brother stumbleth, or is offended,
or is made weak" (Rom. 14: 21).

*57. With what sins does the Apostle Paul place drunk-
enness?*

With idolatry, strife, and murder. (Gal. 5 : 19-21.)

*58. What should we always remember about our
bodies?*

That they are God's temples, and should be kept pure
and clean, fit for him to live in. (I. Cor. 6: 19.)

59. Can the drunkard go to heaven?

"Nor thieves, nor covetous, nor drunkards, nor revilers,
nor extortioners, shall inherit the kingdom of God" (I.
Cor. 6 : 10).

*60. What should be our rule concerning all intoxicating
drinks?*

"Abstain from all appearance of evil" (I. Thes. 5: 22).
"Touch not; taste not; handle not" (Col. 2: 21).

4

CHAPTER X.

PLEDGES.

1. ANTI-SALOON PLEDGE.

REALIZING the evils resulting from the habit and traffic of strong drink, I promise, God helping me, that I will abstain from all intoxicating liquors as a beverage, and will use my influence to induce others to abstain ; that I will do all in my power to abolish drinking-saloons and to prevent the manufacture and sale of intoxicating liquors as a beverage.

2. THE TRIPLE PLEDGE.

I hereby promise, God helping me, to abstain from the use of tobacco in every form, from the use of wine, beer, and other intoxicating drinks, and from the use of all profane and unclean language.

3. ANTI-CIGARETTE PLEDGE.

God being my helper, I do hereby pledge myself, upon honor, to abstain from smoking cigarettes, or using tobacco in any form, and to use my influence and best endeavors to induce others to do the same.

PART V

Supplemental Lessons.

CHAPTER XI.

MEMORY PASSAGES.

1. The Beatitudes.

BLESSED are the poor in spirit : for theirs is the kingdom of heaven.

Blessed are they that mourn : for they shall be comforted.

Blessed are the meek : for they shall inherit the earth.

Blessed are they which do hunger and thirst after righteousness : for they shall be filled.

Blessed are the merciful : for they shall obtain mercy.

Blessed are the pure in heart : for they shall see God.

Blessed are the peacemakers : for they shall be called the children of God.

Blessed are they which are persecuted for righteousness' sake : for theirs is the kingdom of heaven.

2. The First Psalm.

Blessed is the man that walketh not in the counsel of the ungodly, nor standeth in the way of sinners, nor sitteth in the seat of the scornful.

But his delight is in the law of the Lord ; and in his law doth he meditate day and night.

And he shall be like a tree planted by the rivers of water, that bringeth forth his fruit in his season ; his leaf also shall not wither; and whatsoever he doeth shall prosper.

The ungodly are not so : but are like the chaff which the wind driveth away.

Therefore the ungodly shall not stand in the judgment, nor sinners in the congregation of the righteous.

For the Lord knoweth the way of the righteous : but the way of the ungodly shall perish.

3. THE EIGHTH PSALM.

O Lord, our Lord, how excellent is thy name in all the earth! who hast set thy glory above the heavens.

Out of the mouth of babes and sucklings hast thou ordained strength because of thine enemies, that thou mightest still the enemy and the avenger.

When I consider thy heavens, the work of thy fingers, the moon and the stars, which thou hast ordained ;

What is man, that thou art mindful of him? and the son of man, that thou visitest him?

For thou hast made him a little lower than the angels, and hast crowned him with glory and honor.

Thou madest him to have dominion over the works of thy hands ; thou hast put all things under his feet :

All sheep and oxen, yea, and the beasts of the field ;

The fowl of the air, and the fish of the sea, and whatsoever passeth through the paths of the seas.

O Lord, our Lord, how excellent is thy name in all the earth !

4. THE TWENTY-THIRD PSALM.

The Lord is my shepherd ; I shall not want.

He maketh me to lie down in green pastures ; he leadeth me beside the still waters.

He restoreth my soul : he leadeth me in the paths of righteousness for his name's sake.

Yea, though I walk through the valley of the shadow of death, I will fear no evil : for thou art with me ; thy rod and thy staff they comfort me.

Thou preparest a table before me in the presence of mine enemies : thou anointest my head with oil ; my cup runneth over.

Surely goodness and mercy shall follow me all the days of my life : and I will dwell in the house of the Lord for ever.

5. The Love Chapter.

I. Corinthians 13 (R. V.).

If I speak with the tongues of men and of angels, but have not love, I am become sounding brass, or a clanging cymbal.

And if I have the gift of prophecy, and know all mysteries and all knowledge ; and if I have all faith, so as to remove mountains, but have not love, I am nothing.

And if I bestow all my goods to feed the poor, and if I give my body to be burned, but have not love, it profiteth me nothing.

Love suffereth long, and is kind ; love envieth not ; love vaunteth not itself, is not puffed up,

Doth not behave itself unseemly, seeketh not its own, is not provoked, taketh not account of evil ;

Rejoiceth not in unrighteousness, but rejoiceth with the truth ;

Beareth all things, believeth all things, hopeth all things, endureth all things.

Love never faileth : but whether there be prophecies, they shall be done away ; whether there be tongues, they shall cease ; whether there be knowledge, it shall be done away.

For we know in part, and we prophesy in part :

But when that which is perfect is come, that which is in part shall be done away.

But now abideth faith, hope, love, these three ; and the greatest of these is love.

6. The Ten Commandments.

I. Thou shalt have no other gods before me.

II. Thou shalt not make unto thee any graven image, or any likeness of any thing that is in heaven above, or that is in the earth beneath, or that is in the water under the earth : thou shalt not bow down thyself to them, nor serve them : for I the Lord thy God am a jealous God, visiting the iniquity of the fathers upon the children unto the third and fourth generation of them that hate me; and showing mercy unto thousands of them that love me, and keep my commandments.

III. Thou shalt not take the name of the Lord thy God in vain : for the Lord will not hold him guiltless that taketh his name in vain.

IV. Remember the Sabbath day, to keep it holy. Six days shalt thou labor and do all thy work : but the seventh day is the Sabbath of the Lord thy God : in it thou shalt not do any work, thou, nor thy son, nor thy daughter, thy man-servant, nor thy maid-servant, nor thy cattle, nor thy stranger that is within thy gates : for in six days the Lord made heaven and earth, the sea, and all that in them is, and rested the seventh day : wherefore the Lord blessed the Sabbath day, and hallowed it.

V. Honor thy father and thy mother : that thy days may be long upon the land which the Lord thy God giveth thee.

VI. Thou shalt not kill.

VII. Thou shalt not commit adultery.

VIII. Thou shalt not steal.

IX. Thou shalt not bear false witness against thy neighbor.

X. Thou shalt not covet thy neighbor's house, thou shalt not covet thy neighbor's wife, nor his man-servant, nor his maid-servant, nor his ox, nor his ass, nor anything that is thy neighbor's.

7. WISDOM FOR THE YOUNG.

READING FROM THE PROVERBS OF SOLOMON.

Leader. Hear me now therefore, O ye children,

Response. And depart not from the words of my mouth.

L. My son, attend unto my wisdom,

R. And bow thine ear to my understanding ;

L. Lest thou give thine honor unto others,

R. And thy years unto the cruel ;

L. Lest strangers be filled with thy wealth,

R. And thy labors be in the house of a stranger ;

L. And thou mourn at the last,

R. When thy flesh and thy body are consumed,

L. And say, How have I hated instruction,

R. And my heart despised reproof ;

L. And have not obeyed the voice of my teachers,

R. Nor inclined mine ear to them that instructed me !

L. His own iniquities shall take the wicked himself,

R. And he shall be holden with the cords of his sins.

L. He shall die without instruction ;

R. And in the greatness of his folly he shall go astray.

L. My son, attend to my words ;

R. Incline thine ear unto my sayings:

L. Let them not depart from thine eyes ;

R. Keep them in the midst of thine heart :

L. For they are life unto those that find them,

R. And health to all their flesh.

CHAPTER XII.

PRAYERS.

1. THE LORD'S PRAYER.

OUR Father which art in heaven, Hallowed be thy
name. Thy kingdom come. Thy will be done in earth,
as it is in heaven. Give us this day our daily bread.
And forgive us our debts, as we forgive our debtors. And
lead us not into temptation, but deliver us from evil:
For thine is the kingdom, and the power, and the glory,
for ever. Amen.

2. A CHILD'S EVENING PRAYER.

Now I lay me down to sleep,
I pray thee, Lord, my soul to keep;
If I should die before I wake,
I pray thee, Lord, my soul to take.
And this I ask for Jesus' sake. Amen.

3. CHILDHOOD'S PRAYER.

As now I lay me down to sleep,
May angel guards around me keep,
Through all the silent hours of night,
Their watch and ward till morning light.
Dim evening shades around me creep,
As now I lay me down to sleep.
I pray thee, Lord, my soul to keep,
The while I wake or while I sleep;
And while I work and while I play,
I pray thee, Lord, my soul to take:
I pray that thou wouldst for me make
Close at thy feet a lowly place,
Where I may e'er behold thy face,
And this I ask for thy dear sake—

I pray thee, Lord, my soul to take.
Give me thy grace, that, day by day,
Thy love may in my heart grow deep,
I pray thee, Lord, my soul to keep.
If I should die before I wake ;
If I this night the world forsake,
And leave the friends I hold most dear,
Leave all that I so value here ;
And if thy call my slumbers break—
If I should die before I wake,
While bending at my mother's knee,
This little prayer she taught to me—
"Now as I lay me down to sleep,
I pray thee, Lord, my soul to keep ;
If I should die before I wake,
I pray thee, Lord, my soul to take."

—*Newton S. Otis.*

4. An Evening Prayer.

Now the light has gone away,
Saviour, listen while I pray,
Asking thee to watch and keep,
And to send me quiet sleep.

Jesus, Saviour, wash away
All that has been wrong to-day ;
Help me ev'ry day to be
Good and gentle, more like thee.

Let my near and dear ones be
Always near and dear to thee ;
Oh, bring me and all I love
To thy happy home above.

Thou my best and kindest friend,
Thou wilt love me to the end !
Let me love thee more and more,
Always better than before.

—*Frances Ridley Havergal.*

5. A Morning Prayer.

O Lord, I give thee thanks that thou hast taken care of me the past night, and that I am permitted to see the light of another morning. Keep me, O Lord, from evil all this day, and may I love and serve thee with a true heart always. Grant me, I pray thee, every good thing which I need for my body and soul. Create in me a clean heart, and help me by thy Holy Spirit to do thy will. Be merciful to me and forgive my sins. So help me every day that I may please thee in all things. This I ask for Christ's sake. Amen.

6. An Evening Prayer.

Heavenly Father, I bow down before thee to give thee thanks for all the blessings of this day. Thou hast been very near to me and hast been very good. Thou hast supplied all my needs and hast kept me from all harm. Forgive me the sins of this day, I pray thee, and keep me always in thy love. Watch over me while I sleep, and may no evil thing come to me. Bless all my near and dear friends. May they all be ever dear to thee. Bless the sad and the poor and the needy. Help them always to place their hands in thine and to go only where thou leadest. May I always be kind to the troubled and ever be like thy dear Son, my Saviour, who went about doing good. These mercies I ask for his name's sake. Amen.

APPENDIX.

MODEL CONSTITUTION FOR A JUNIOR YOUNG PEOPLE'S SOCIETY.

THE following model constitution is presented to the Church as embracing the leading features necessary to successful Christian work among boys and girls. Verbal changes may be made to adapt it to the wants of a given church or community. There may be more or fewer committees, as local needs may require.

The success of any Junior society and its work will depend chiefly on the leaders and the pastor. On them will devolve the task of adapting the organization to local conditions and circumstances. The leaders should be earnest Christian workers with a special love for work among boys and girls.

CONSTITUTION. [1]

ARTICLE I.

Name.

This organization shall be known as the Junior Young People's Society of ——— United Brethren Church of ———.

ARTICLE II.

Object.

The object of this society shall be to promote in its members a pure and worthy character, to aid in the study of the Bible, and to cultivate the principles of loyal service to Christ.

[1] Copies of this constitution may be had at three cents each by addressing the United Brethren Publishing House, Dayton, Ohio. If a constitution for a Junior Christian Endeavor society is desired, it can be had at the same rates.

ARTICLE III.

Membership.

SECTION 1. The members shall be boys and girls from seven to fifteen years of age, who shall have been approved by the leaders, and elected by a majority vote of the members present at any regular meeting.

SEC. 2. All those who become members shall pledge [1] themselves to attend regularly the meetings of the society and to observe good order in them.

ARTICLE IV.

Officers.

SECTION 1. The officers of this society shall be a leader and an assistant leader (adults), a president, vice-president, secretary, and treasurer.

SEC. 2. The leaders shall be nominated by the young people's society of the church (or by the teachers and officers of the Sunday school where no young people's society exists), and their nomination shall be approved by the pastor and the official board.

[1] This pledge should be understood to be taken by all members received into the society. Where a more formal pledge is desired, the following may be adopted :

JUNIOR SOCIETY PLEDGE.

Trusting in Jesus Christ to help me, I promise that I will strive to do whatever he would like to have me do; that I will pray and read the Bible, and keep the Sabbath day holy; and that just so far as I know how I will try to lead a good life; that I will be present at every meeting when not hindered by sickness or some other just cause; and that I will take some part in the meetings, especially the monthly recognition meetings.

NOTE.—There should be great care taken in having young children, who will innocently sign anything, take this pledge. The pledge should be clearly explained and wisely emphasized. To secure the coöperation of parents the leaders should send them a copy of the pledge, and also the following for the parent to sign :

PARENT'S ANSWER.

I have carefully read the accompanying pledge and cheerfully give my consent for .... to sign it, and will do what I can to help .... to faithfully keep it.

Parent's Name ....

Address ....

ARTICLE V.

Duties of Officers.

SECTION 1. The leader shall have general charge of the society and its work.

SEC. 2. The assistant leader shall aid the leader at his request, and care for all the funds received from the treasurer.

SEC. 3. The president shall preside at all business meetings, under the advice of the leader.

SEC. 4. The vice-president shall conduct business meetings in the absence of the president.

SEC. 5. The secretary shall keep a record of the names and attendance of members, and of the proceedings of all business meetings.

SEC. 6. The treasurer shall take the collections, enter the amount in a book provided for that purpose, and turn over the money to the assistant leader for safe keeping. A record shall also be kept of all expenditures, as directed by the leader and society.

ARTICLE VI.

Committees.

There shall be five standing committees of five (or three, as may be desired) members each, as follows,— the members in each (except the executive committee) to be proposed by the leaders and approved by the society :

1. *Membership.* To bring in those who may wish to become members, to introduce them to the leaders, and to help them to feel at home in the meetings of the society.

2. *Devotional.* To help the leader to arrange programs, provide music, to distribute Bibles, singing books, tracts, etc., and to aid in every way which the leaders may direct to promote the interest of the meetings.

3. *Helping-Hand.* To seek new scholars for the Sunday school, and to bring them in and introduce them to the superintendent, to visit members when sick or neglectful of the meetings, and to act as special aids to the leaders in securing a full attendance at the monthly recognition service.

4. *Temperance.* To canvass for signatures to the temperance pledge[1] under the direction of the leaders, and to help in any other way to promote temperance work among boys and girls.

5. *Executive Committee.* The pastor, leaders, and the officers shall compose the executive committee, which shall have full control of the affairs of the society.

ARTICLE VII.

Meetings.

SECTION 1. A devotional meeting shall be held every week, the exercises of which shall consist of prayers, Scripture reading and study, singing, and testimony.

SEC. 2. Once a month the meeting shall be known as a recognition meeting. At some time during the exercises the pledge, if there is one, shall be recited in concert, and the roll called. The responses shall be considered a renewal of the pledge of the society. The name of any member who is absent without excuse from four consecutive recognition meetings shall be dropped from the roll of members.

SEC. 3. All meetings shall be in charge of the leaders. If there are those among the members capable of leading meetings, they may be chosen to do so.

SEC. 4. The pastor or leaders shall use a part of the hour of the weekly meeting, when deemed best, for special instruction in Bible truth, or for other profitable exercises.

ARTICLE VIII.

Relationship.

This society shall be considered a department of the church with which it is connected. It shall also sustain a close and intimate relation to the young people's society of the church, with which the members of this junior society are expected to connect themselves when they have reached the age limit.

[1] See Triple Pledge, p. 50.

BY-LAWS.

SECTION 1. The regular meetings of this society shall be held on Sunday afternoon of each week.[1] The last meeting of each month shall be a recognition meeting. The business meeting shall be held in connection with the first meeting of each month.

SEC. 2. The leaders, in consultation with the pastor, shall at each election propose names of available members for the several offices, who shall be elected by a majority vote of the members present. The officers shall be elected and the committees appointed for a term of six months, and shall enter upon their duties the ——— day of ——— and the ——— day of ——— of each year.

SEC. 3. The funds for the expenses of the society and other purposes shall be raised by collections taken at the monthly recognition meetings, and at other meetings as the leaders may arrange.

SEC. 4. Special meetings of the society may be called at any time by the pastor or leaders.

SEC. 5. The committees should hold a meeting with the leaders once a month for consultation about their work.

SEC. 6. Other committees may be appointed at any time as they may be needed.

SEC. 7. This constitution and by-laws may be amended at any regular meeting upon the recommendation of the executive committee.

[1] Or at the discretion of the pastor and leaders. In country churches and during the heated term, in summer, it may not be practicable to hold weekly meetings.

www.ingramcontent.com/pod-product-compliance
Lightning Source LLC
Chambersburg PA
CBHW021529090426
42739CB00007B/849